THE OLYMPIC GAMES IN ANTIQUITY

TINA ZISSIMOU
Archeologist

Introduction

Sports of different kinds are a phenomenon, the roots of which can be traced back to many oriental people as early as the 3rd millenium BC. Archeological research has shown that the Assyrians, the Sumerians, the Babylonians and in particular the Egyptians practiced various sports, some of which were very popular. In all these cases, however, these sports were games, the purpose of which was to amuse the participants rather than to serve an ideal. In contrast, in ancient Greece athleticism was not only a part of the every day life of the inhabitants but also an indispensable part of education with the aim of creating citizens for the democracy rather than just strong and efficient soldiers. This is a unique phenomenon in world history, which first appears in ancient Greece and disappears together with its decline. Consequently it is not without reason that this country is considered to be the birthplace of the athletic ideal.

In the Hellenic world, sports were already known in Minoan Crete but it was the Myceneans who gave them their purely athletic character. Being good warriors with heroic ideals, they were just the people to improve the various contests in a society with a competitive spirit. They inspired the simple foot race but also the most aristocratic event, the chariot races. Wrestling and boxing are of Mycenean origin too. The archery, the discus, the arms drill contests and the javelin, that are mentioned by Homer, may also date back to the period of the decline of the Mycenean era. The latest event to be added must have been the long jump, as it is mentioned only in the Odyssey

Young boxers with boxing handshoes. Wall painting from Thera. 15th century BC (Athens, National Archaeological Museum).

7

and not in the Iliad.

The origin of the games and their relation to those of the prehistoric period is a subject that is still under discussion among scholars. The most probable theory seems to be the one connecting the classical athletic games with those held in honour of dead heroes as a funeral rite, and were closely related to religion. The description of such funeral games by Homer in the Iliad, after the death of Patroclus, the best friend of Achilles, is widely known. The custom of honouring dead heroes with funeral games survived throughout antiquity in parallel with the regular athletic contests. It can be found, in the classical era, after the battles of Marathon, Plataea and Leuctra and also, in the 4th century BC, when Alexander the Great organized games in order to honour his deceased friend Hephaistion. The ancient Greeks believed that athletes took strength from the dead heroes, in whose honour they used to fight and that afterwards they would be able to mirror their feats.

The competitive spirit of the ancient Greeks was naturally reflected in mythology, where we very often find gods and heroes taking part in all kinds of games and receiving a wide variety of rewards. Zeus fought with Kronos for his kingdom and Apollo won the foot race against Hermes and the boxing match against Ares. In memory of these victories of the god of music, the playing of his sacred instrument, the **aulos** (flute), was inaugurated during the physical exercise.

In many cases the athletic events were a means of choosing a husband or wife. Penelope was given to Ulysses as a wife after he had defeated the other suitors and she was about to choose a new husband in the same way having been convinced that Ulysses was dead. Pelops too, married Hippodameia after his victory over her father Oinomaos in the chariot races.

The Olympic Games that this book deals with were the most important of the four sacred **panhellenic** athletic festivals of antiquity. The other three were the Pythian, the Nemean and the Isthmian Games that were respectively held in Delphi, Nemea and Isthmia. The name **panhellenic** (for all the Greeks), explains the participation in them of Greeks from all the Greek cities, while the fact that they took place at powerful religious centres, reflects the aim of these

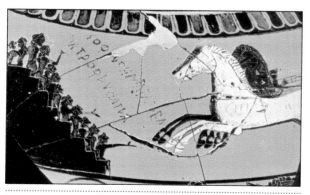

games, which was to forge the links of the common blood, language and religion of all these people. It is thus obvious how huge their contribution to the creation of a uniform classical Greek culture was, and the orator Lysias was right when he wrote in 338 BC: "Hercules founded the games in order to mark the beginning of a mutual friendship among the Greeks".

Depiction of the chariot races held in honour of Patroclos (Athens, National Archaeological Museum).

The legends

The enormous fame the Olympic Games had acquired in the ancient world justifies the creation of many legends to explain their foundation and relate them to important mythological figures.

Such a case is the legend of Pelops. Oinomaos was the King of Pissa and had a beautiful daughter named Hippodameia. He did not, however, allow her to get married because according to an oracle he would be killed by her husband. So he obliged every young man who wanted to marry his daughter to take part in chariot races and only if he won would he then be permitted to become Hippodameia's husband, otherwise he would be killed. The winner of the races was, of course, always the old king because the horses of his chariot were a present from the god Poseidon and were "faster than the north wind". Thirteen suitors had already been killed when Pelops arrived in Pisa. He was a very handsome young man and the king's daughter fell in love with him. Thus, before the games she persuaded her father's charioteer to replace the wooden axle pin of the king's chariot with another one made of wax. Naturally, during the races the wax melted and the king fell from his chariot and was killed. Pelops was proclaimed the winner, married Hippodameia and gave his name to the Peloponnese. After his victory, he organized chariot races as thanksgiving to the gods or as funeral games in honour of Oinomaos, in order to be purified of his death. For a similar reason his wife, Hippodameia, founded the simple track races for women, the so-called Heraia.

According to another legend, the greatest hero of Greece, Hercules, coming back from one of his labours, the cleaning of the stables of King Augeus, founded the games at the place where Pelop's tomb was located and planted the olive tree, the branches of which were used

Pelops and Hippodameia on a quadriga (four-horse chariot) (Arezzo, Museo Archeologico).

The stadium of Olympia. View from the West. On the left the altar of Demeter Chamyne, on the right the podium of the Hellanodikai and in the foreground the finish line.

The Krypte. The covered official entrance to the stadium.

to crown the winners (Pind. Olymp. 10.23-31).

Another Hercules ,the one from Ida, is also mentioned as being the founder of the games. He first fixed the length of the stadium in Olympia, then had his brothers, the Kourites, run and then crowned the winner with an olive branch. And because his brothers were five in number, he settled that the games would take place every fifth year.

The theory closest to the truth must be the one mentioned by Strabo, that the games were organized by the Herakleides, Hercules' descendants, who came to Elis under the command of Ochylos and that they were revamped by his descendant Iphitos, who also imposed the institution of the Olympic Truce.

Depiction of the wrestling between Hercules and Antaios (Paris, the Louvre).

O lympia is located at an altitude of 60m., in a valley surrounded by small hills and by two rivers, the Alpheios and the Kladeos, which, in antiquity were worshipped as divinities and the statues of which decorated the East pediment of the temple of Zeus.

Archeological research has clearly proved that the area has been inhabited since 2800 BC but it is most probable that it started being used as a sanctuary at the end of the Mycenean period (12th century BC). As in all the areas around the Mediterranean, we find in the prehistory of Olympia a matriarchal society with the dominant divinity generally known as **Gaia,** the goddess of the fertility of the earth. This female divinity was later replaced by a male, the father of both man and the gods, Zeus, who remained the main divinity of the sanctuary till the end of antiquity.

The beginning of the games at Olympia is lost in prehistory and the ancient sources are too contradictory to be able to help us find the end of the thread. They all mention however the sanctuary as the theatre of a certain fight among some gods or heroes and one of them as being the founder of the Games. It is probable that athletic games were already being held at Olympia in the 10th century BC but from the 8th century and more precisely from 776 BC the results of the games, that is the names of the winners, were written down on lists that were called Olympic Lists. These lists are, for the archaeologists, a valuable source of information as they were, for the ancient Greeks, the basis of their time counting system. Almost every ancient Greek city-state had its own system for counting time that had as its starting point a very important event, such as the fall of Troy, or the beginning of the reign of a sovereign, or, as in the classical period, one based on a list of **archontes** (dignitaries) of that year. The system of dating according to the Olympiads had the advantage that it was common to all Greeks who were very well aware when the Olympic Games took place. Every Olympiad was named after the winner of the simple sprint race. The first winner mentioned was Koroibos, a cook from the town of Elis. This chronological system was in use till the 4th century BC. It is worth noting that the year 776 BC is the earliest verifiable date in the history of Western Civilization.

In the first centuries of its history, the sanctuary of Olympia was nothing but an area surrounded by a low wall with a few simple buildings, altars and memorials to heroes, a grove as its name **Altis** (grove) indicates, full of planetrees, wild olives, pines, oaks and elms. The games that were held there were still of a local character and did not yet have the glamour that they later enjoyed. The organization of the games was originally under the control of Pissa, a small town located 5-6 km. from Olympia. When they started becoming famous, the town of Elis, although located about 50 km. from the sanctu-

When the games were held - The truce

*T*he games at Olympia were held in the middle of the summer, after a period of four full years was completed, which was in accordance with the calendar system used by other **panhellenic** games. The period of four years was half of the eight-year period of Cleostratus, that is of a period of time in which the difference of 11 1\4 days between the lunar year of 354 days and the solar year of 365 1\4 days was corrected. Originally the year was divided into 12 months of 28 days each, but there proved to be a discrepancy with the actual seasons and so they were obliged, every eight years, to insert three additional months. The Olympic Games were held on the first full moon after the summer solstice, that is between 15th July and 15th August. The period between the end of the games and the beginning of the next ones was called Olympiad, a term that is also used for the Olympic Games themselves. Every Olympiad was named after the winner of the **stadion**, that is the sprint race.

For the first time, at around 400 BC, the sophist Hippias from Elia drew up a list of the Olympic Games, based on research carried out in the archives of the sanctuary and on hearsay. His numbering started, conventionally, from the year 776 BC, when Koroibos from Elis was crowned as the winner. This date is also consistent with the beginning of the historic period in Greece. Later other writers, such as Aristotle, Eratosthenes, Phlegon and Julius the African also occupied themselves with revising and completing the lists. Even later, Timeus from Sicily (352 - 256 BC) or Eratosthenes (275 - 195 BC) used these numbered Olympiads for the measuring of time. This chronological system was later adopted by historians like Diodorus from Sicily, Polybius, Dionysios from Alicarnassos etc. replacing the local chronological methods (in Athens they used to date according to the **eponymoi archontes**, in Argos according to the priestesses of Hera etc.).

Shortly before the beginning of the games, delegates from Elis, the so-called **spondophoroi**, crowned with olive wreaths and holding staffs, left Olympia in order to announce to all the Greek cities the beginning of the sacred Truce, which originally lasted only one month but was extended, after the 5th century BC to three months, starting from the day of their departure. During the Truce, any hostilities between Greek cities were interrupted. The aim of this sacred peace was to ensure the security of the games in Olympia itself, as it prohibited any attack against it as well as ensuring the safe journey of the tens of thousands of spectators to and from all parts of the then known world, wherever there were Greek cities. Greeks travelled to Olympia not only from present day Greek territory but also from the colonies, which were spread out all over the Mediterranean. Many of today's cities such as Naples, Regio and Taranto on the mainland of Italy, Syracuse, Agrigento, Segesta in Sicily, Marseilles in France, Alexandria in Egypt, Ephesus Pergamon, Milet, Alicarnassos, Byzantion (later called Constantinople) in Turkey, Odessa and Yalta on the Black Sea, just to mention a few, were Greek colonies, from which athletes as well as spectators sped, in order to take part in the greatest athletic festival of the ancient world.

A violation of the Truce was considered as disrespect to the god, in honour of whom the games were held. Characteristic of the holiness with which they were surrounded are the various ancient traditions, which although contradictory, attribute the original establishment of the Truce to a demigod, such as Hercules, or to a legendary legislator, such as Lycurgus from Sparta. Pausanias mentions that in Olympia among the other offerings, he saw the discus of Iphitos, a person of doubtful historical existence, on which the conditions of the truce were engraved. They were:

1. the interruption of all hostilities among the Greek cities
2. the prohibition of the entrance in Olympia to anyone who carried weapons
3. the suspension of the execution of the death penalty.

Pausanias also saw, on the right side of the entrance to the temple of Zeus, a statue of Zeus "being crowned by the Truce ", obviously a pictorial personification of the sacred peace. Nevertheless, despite the sacred character of the Truce, the importance of the games was so great for the Greeks that they would not risk their safe execution. The episode concerning King Philip II, Alexander the Great's father, who paid a penalty and was made to apologize because one of his mercenaries prevented the Athenian Phrynon from going to Olympia in order to watch the games (Thucyd. 5.49), is indicative of the importance given to the truce.

During the long history of the games very few cases of violation of the Truce occurred, a fact which proves the respect and the prestige that surrounded this institution.

The nudity of the athletes

*I*n order to understand the fact that the athletes in ancient Greece took part in the games quite naked, it must be regarded as a philosophical phenomenon that appeared for the first time in Greek culture and that it was incomprehensible to the **barbarians**, who related nudity with immorality. The Greeks, in contrast to other ancient people, regarded the human body with awe and respect, considering it to be the incarnation of two concepts the one of the athlete and the one of the hero. This abstract dimension of the nude is especially clear in ancient Greek art, in sculpture, wall painting or vase painting.

It is a fact that this attitude to the nude is not to be found in the early periods of Greek history. In the Mycenean period, according to Homer's description, the athletes in some of the funeral games held in honour of Patroclos wore a so called "zoma".

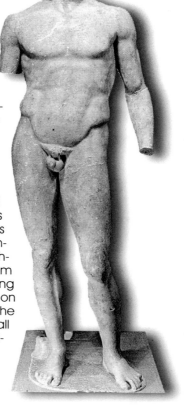

Thucydides mentions that the Spartans were the first ones to inaugurate the nudity of the athletes in the games and that it had occurred a few years before his era, whereas up until then the athletes would wear belts around their genital organs. According to another tradition, mentioned by Pausanias, the first athlete who ran nude at Olympia was Orsippus from Megara, in the 15th Olympics (720 B. C). During the race the athletes zoma fell off, but he kept on running and even finished first. According to the same writer, the runner purposely let his dress fall in order to run faster. An inscription from the Hellenistic period that was found on his tomb in Megara confirms that he was the first winner in Olympia who was crowned nude. Nevertheless, some vases from the end of the 6th

Roman copy of a statue by Lysippos, depicting the famous pankration winner Agias, who lived in the 5th century BC (Delphi, Archaeological Museum).

Scene of wrestling. The athletes wear a zoma (Rome, Musei Vaticani).

century BC depict athletes wearing a white loincloth. It is thus probable that complete nudity originally concerned only some sports, for example the track races, and that it was extended from the 5th century BC to the others, or that perhaps, at around the end of the 6th century BC an attempt was made to abolish nudity that did not finally succeed. It was probably this attempt that Thucydides and Plato had in mind when they said that the nudity of the athletes began shortly before their time.

The fact that the athletic games were linked with nudity also becomes clear from the etymology of the words **gymnasion** (gymnasium) and gymnastic, that derive from the Greek word **gymnos** (nude).

It should be noted that after 338 BC due to the incident with Kallipateira, daughter of the Olympic winner Diagoras, who had watched the games disguised as a trainer, it was decreed that trainers should also be naked in the stadium during the games.

The gymnasiums

*T*he word **gymnasion** (gymnasium), which in most of European languages means school, derives from the Greek word **gymnos** (nude) and means a place were nude men train. The gymnasiums were public buildings, usually surrounded by porticoes and with a big open air courtyard in the centre, where there were areas for the accommodation and the training of the athletes, for the jumping pit, for the wrestling and the boxing, a place for the throws, an open air track for the races, changing rooms and also, after the 5th century BC, a library, conference halls etc. The gymnasiums were places where not only the young men but also the great men of ancient Greece, orators and philosophers, would spend their time, talking about the political, religious and philosophical problems of their times. So, in time, these places became the real schools of antiquity and the word gymnasium became synonymous with the word school. And it is not the only word that has to do with education that derives from the field of the ancient athletics. The word **Lykeion** (Lyceum) which also means school today, was the name of such a gymnasium in Athens, dedicated to the hero Lykeios, where Aristotle used to teach. The word **Academia** (Academy), which worldwide means an educational institution, was the name of an other Athenian gymnasium, dedicated to the hero Academos, and it was there that the philosophical school of Plato was situated. It is obvious, through the etymology of these words, how important for the ancient Greeks the ideal of « a healthy mind in a healthy body » was, and that athletics in antiquity used to have a spiritual character, which unfortunately has been lost for ever.

Scene in the Palaistra. The muscles of an athlete are being massaged by a helping personel. On the right stands his trainer (Rome, Villa Giulia).

Scene in the palaistra. In the centre, an athlete is about to smear his body with the oil that he pours out of a small vase (Berlin, Staatliche Museen).

Conditions of participation
- Preliminary period

*I*n order to have the right to participate in the Olympic Games one had to be Greek, male and a free citizen: that is **barbarians**, women and slaves were excluded.

Athletes who wanted to take part had to register within a pre-determined time limit, otherwise they paid a penalty or were even excluded. Pausanias mentions the case of Apollonius from Alexandria, who did not arrive within the fixed time limit and the Elians were obliged, according to the rules, to exclude him from the games. His excuse that he was delayed in the Cyclades islands by adverse winds was proved false by Herakleides, who had also arrived at Olympia from Alexandria.

The athletes had to be in Elis one month before the beginning of the games, during which time they trained under the supervision of the **Hellanodikai**, while their trainers were obliged to be present. The training in Elis was very hard and the athletes had to obey the orders of the **Hellanodikai**, who if opposed could punish them with a flogging or even exclusion from the games. This preliminary period did not have the same significance as preliminary games in their modern form as it was not simply a physical but also a mental test. During this preparation the **Hellanodikai** judged the character and the morality of the athletes, their power, resistance and endurance and generally their ability to perform in front of a **panhellenic** audience at a level in keeping with the fame and the history of the sanctuary.

Two days before the beginning of the festival, those who would finally participate left Elis in order to go to Olympia, along the Sacred Road, in a procession at the head of which were the **Hellanodikai** and the officials.

The Hellanodikes

*T*he institution of the judge who was responsible for the execution of the games and the announcing of the winners, was closely connected with the existence of the games themselves. From Homer we know that Achilles was the judge of the funeral games which he had himself organized, in honour of his friend Patroclus and that was also the case of Hercules, Pelops and the king Iphitos, in the sanctuary of Olympia itself. We can then conclude that originally it was the organizers of the games who supervised their execution. And as only persons of high standing, in those times mainly kings, would be able to afford the organization of such an event, it is obvious that the purple garb which the judges have been wearing throughout the history of the games is due to the royal origin of the institution (Philostr. Gymn. 11, 54).

The name of the high judges of the games, **Hellanodikes**, that is judges of the Greeks, emphasizes the exclusively Greek origin of the participants. In the beginning their was only one **Hellanodikai**. In 580 BC (the 50th Olympiad) a second one was added and later their number was increased to nine. Three of them supervised the **pentathlon**, three the events of the horse racing and three the rest of the games. This number varied however, until 348 BC (the 108th Olympiad) when it was stabilized at ten, which then applied until the end of the games. Dur-

A judge supervises two pankration athletes (Paris, the Louvre).

ing the first centuries the office was for life and hereditary, but from the 6th century BC and in line with wider political and social changes, they were elected from all the citizens of Elis.

The **Hellanodikai** were elected by the drawing of lots for each Olympiad, and one member from each tribe of the area was drawn. For ten months before the beginning of the games, they lived in the **Hellanodikaion**, a building especially constructed for this purpose in the **Agora** (marketplace) of Elis and close to one of the gymnasiums that stood there. During their stay the **Hellanodikai** were taught by the **nomophylakes** (guardians of the law) the regulations and the provisions of the

Athlete of the pentathlon. Besides the discus the halteres for the jump are also depicted. The athlete is marking with a wooden nail the length of the throw. Behind him a pickaxe for the digging of the sand in the sandpit (Paris, the Louvre).

games. In the last month before the games, they watched the training of the athletes and classified them into four categories, according to their age (Paus. 6.23.2). This classification was rather difficult considering that at this time there were no official certificates which would prove their date of birth. During the month of the training of the athletes under the supervision of the **Hellanodikai** their trainers were not allowed to interfere under penalty of flogging. The **Hellanodikai** did not judge only the physical condition of the athletes but also their behavior. Those that were not considered to be properly prepared were excluded from the games.

When the preparatory stage and the preliminary assessment of the athletes were over, the **Hellanodikai** joined an official procession to the sanctuary of Olympia, where they were in general command. They sometimes fixed the running order of the events, decided in case of a tie between of the athletes and imposed physical or monetary penalties on those who violated the regulations. They could also exclude athletes during the course of the games. A characteristic case of punishment with the whip happened in the Olympics of 420 BC during the Peloponnesian War, when the Spartans were punished with a penalty of 2000 mnai and exclusion from the games, because they had broken the sacred Truce. The Spartan Lichas, nevertheless took part in the chariot races, registering his **synoris** as being from Thebes. But during the award ceremony he himself tied the victory rosette around the forehead of his charioteer, wishing to show everybody that the chariot was his own. The **Hellanodikai** then had him whipped. As for the victory, it was registered not for Sparta but for Thebes. In spite of this Lichas was allowed to erect his statue in the **Altis** as all the winners used to do (Paus. 6.2.2-3 , Xenoph. Hellen. 3,2,21).

Another duty of the **Hellanodikai** was to check if the contestants had been registered before the games began, in the special list called **leukoma**. A penalty was also imposed on those who, having been registered, then with-

A Hellanodikes with a palm branch and a pentathlete with the discus (Paris, the Louvre).

26

drew from the games that had already started, without any serious reason. Such a rare case is that of Theagenes from Thasos, who had been registered to participate in the boxing and in the **pankration**, but because after the first contest he was already exhausted, he was not able to fight in the second too. For his absence he was punished with a fine of 2 talanta.

Besides the imposing of penalties, the **Hellanodikai** had the most honourable duty of the coronation of the winners.

All the decisions of the **Hellanodikai** were irrevocable. If an athlete had the impression that he had been misjudged, he could have recourse to the **Boule** of the Elians, which, during the games, was in session in the_**Bouleuterion** of Olympia. This council could punish a **Hellanodikes** for a wrong decision, but it did not have the right to cancel it. This was the case of Eupolemos, a **stadion** runner from Elis, when two of the three **Hellanodikai** decided in his favor, while the third one regarded Leon from Ambrakia as the winner. The latter, believing that he had been a victim of injustice, resorted to the **Boule** of the Elians, which finally ruled in his favor. The two **Hellanodikai** were fined for their wrong judgement, but Eupolemos remained the winner and he even erected his statue in the sanctuary (Paus. 6.3.7).

The authority of the **Hellanodikai** was enormous as was the trust that the Greeks had in them. The incident just mentioned is the unique case in the more than one thousand-year old history of the games which could be considered as partiality of the **Hellanodikai** in favor of a fellow citizen. And in order to avoid any suspicious of non-impartial judgment, from 332 BC (the 112th Olympiad), after the victories of a judge in the chariot races, the participation of the **Hellanodikai** in any event was prohibited.

In the execution of their duties the **Hellanodikai** were assisted by the floggers and the **alytes,** an actual police corps which were under the command of a superior, the **alytarches**. Besides them, there were various personnel with specialized duties: those who were responsible for the sacrifices, a person that played the flute during the sacrifices, one responsible for the wood, another who announced the participation of the athletes in the games, a person who gave an explanation to the visitors about the games, as well as a doctor and an architect. There were also secondary personnel that consisted of the **oinochoos** (vintner), the **kleidouchos** (key-keeper), the cooks, the caretakers etc.

The feeding of the athletes

*I*n the first centuries of antiquity the athletes did not make any special kind of preparation for the games nor did they train systematically nor follow any particular diet. Their food, in common with the rest of the Greeks consisted mainly of bread, cheese, milk, olives, olive oil, vegetables, fruits and small quantities of fish and meat. But from the beginning of the 5th century BC we have information about certain athletes who varied their diet in order to achieve better results. The most common tendency was the replacement of several foods, mainly cheese, with meat (Paus. 6.7.10). The introduction of large quantities of meat to the diet of the athletes caused a unprecedented change in their weight and muscular strength, especially of those who practiced heavy disciplines, in which, as we know, there was no division into categories according to weight. In addition they started training harder, which had as a result the need for more hours for rest and sleep. Their life became so centred on the triptych of training, food, sleep that they did not have time for other activities. This specialization developed to such an extent, that already in the times of Plato we meet the term " medical gymnastic" that is, the active involvement of the science of medicine in sports, and later even the existence of specialized dietitians and cooks, who were involved with the improvement of the physical condition of the athletes.

Such a disturbance to the balance between the cultivation of the physical and the mental could not but draw the criticism of the intellectuals of the times. Not only Socrates (Xenoph. Apomn. 1.2.4) but also Aristotle (Polit. 1139a) and Athenaios (10. 413) declared their opposition to this practice which was inconsistent, not only with the beauty of the body but also with the idea of moderation in all things, which constituted the fundamental philosophy of the times.

The programme of an Olympiad

*T*he duration of the Olympic Games fluctuated over the centuries. In the beginning they lasted only one day, because there were not many contests and participation was restricted. In 472 BC (the 76th Olympiad), because of the delay caused by the **pentathlon** in the previous games the **Hellanodikai** decided that the games should last longer, but we do not know by how many days (Paus. 5.9.3). This number of days was probably increased progressively. The fact is that it was finally fixed at five days. The exact programme of the games is not known. Besides, with the addition and subtraction of events there would be changes from time to time, but we can get a general impression of an Olympiad around the 4th century BC when most of the events had been included in the programme. It should be noted that the **Hellanodikai** had the right to change, even at the last moment, the order of the events, if they considered it necessary. Such a thing happened in 212 BC (the

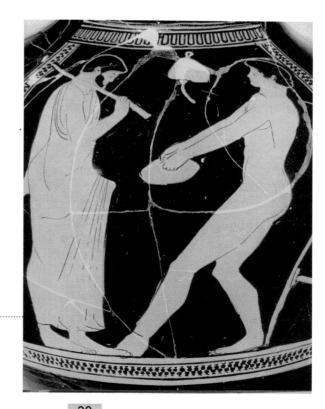

Athlete training in the jump under the supervision of the trainer (Würzburg, Martin von Wagner Museum).

142nd Olympiad) when, as an exception, the **pankration** was held before the boxing, so that an athlete who would take part in both events would be in good condition during the second, since boxing was regarded as a much harder event.

Already before the beginning of the games a huge crowd of tens of thousands had arrived at Olympia from all over Greece and had settled down in the valley around the sanctuary. Most of them slept in tents or simply in the open air, a few officials in guest houses like the

Athlete jumping with the help of a pair of halteres (Heidelberg, Archäologisches Institut der Universität).

Leonidaion , a luxurious lodge, the ruins of which are still preserved. Together with the spectators a considerable number of professionals and traders arrived at Olympia, who supplied them with food and refreshments.

The first day of every Olympiad was dedicated to the gods. Early in the morning the procession that had started, two days earlier, from Elis arrived at Olympia. It was lead by the **Hellanodikai** and the priests, followed by the authorities of the city, the official delegations of the other Greek cities, the athletes, the trainers and the child-athletes accompanied by their fathers and brothers.

The first ceremony was the official oath-taking in the **Bouleuterion,** in front of the statue of Orkios Zeus (Zeus protector of the oath). There, in front of the statue, they sacrificed a wild boar and the athletes took an oath, on its genitals, that they would abide by the rules of the games. A similar oath was taken by the trainers, the fathers and the brothers of the athletes, as well as by the judges. Then there was the official registration of the athletes who would participate, as well as their classification into categories according to their age, and the names were announced on the **leukoma** outside the **Bouleuterion.** Sacrifices then followed on the big altar of Zeus and on the six double altars that Hercules had founded, as well as libations on the tomb of Pelops. On the same day, the contests of the trumpeters and the heralds were held. The winners would have the honour of offering their services during the games. These contests had nothing to do with music. The winner was the one whose voice or trumpet would carry the furthest. These contests took place in front of an altar, next to the entrance to the stadium.

On the second day, in a stadium already overcrowded from the time of sunrise, the games began. The **Hellanodikai** in procession and holding branches of palm entered first, followed by the children, who would compete on this day. The trumpeter sounded the trumpet and the herald declared the starting of the games. The athletes drew lots to decide in which lane they would run or against whom they would fight. The first event to be held was the **stadion** and it was followed by the wrestling, the boxing and the **pankration**. After the end of every contest, the winners received branches of palm from the **Hellanodikai**.

The third day was the most impressive because it was dedicated to the races. The chariot and the horse races finished at noon and in the afternoon the **pentathlon** for men was held in the stadium.

The fourth day, which coincided with the full moon, started with the biggest sacrifice of the games, the **hecatombe**, that is the offering of one hundred oxen by the Elians on the big altar of Zeus. Of the animals that were slaughtered in front of the altar, only the legs were

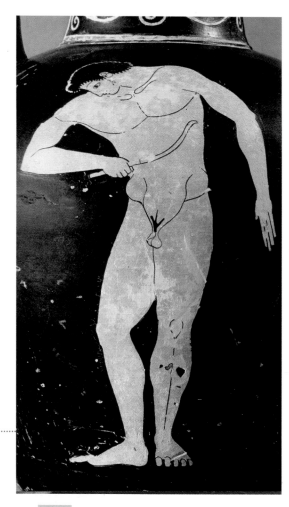

Depiction of an athlete cleaning his body from the oil and the dust with the stlegis (Vienna, Kunsthistorisches Museum).

burned. Afterwards the men's events were held. First the **stadion** and then the **diaulos**, the **dolichos**, the wrestling, the boxing and the **pankration**. The day, as well as the Olympiad, closed with the **hoplites**. During this race, the contestants carried a shield and a helmet, which symbolized that the truce was about to come to an end.

On the fifth day the winners, holding palm branches, gathered in the temple of Zeus, where the most senior of the **Hellanodikai** crowned them with the kotinos, the wreath of the wild olive tree. At noon the Elians served the winners an official meal in the **Prytaneion**, where they arrived in procession singing hymns, while in the evening the winners were honoured with banquets offered by the delegations of the cities and wealthy spectators. The Olympic Games were over.

A discus thrower (Rome, Musei Vaticani).

The events

The track races

These, as is to be expected, are the oldest events of the Olympics, since running constitutes for man the most natural kind of exercise. For this reason its importance in the programme of the games remained great throughout antiquity. It is therefore also to be expected that the ancient Greeks attributed its origin to various mythological figures, such as Hercules. Endymion etc.

The running event is mentioned already by Homer in the Iliad, in the games that Achilles organized in honour of his deceased friend, Patroclus. The winner was Ulysses, who received as a prize a cup from Sidon, and second was Ajax. Ulysses had also won another race and so had been allowed to marry Penelope. In a similar way other kings had chosen husbands for their daughters. Generally, the ability to run fast was regarded by the ancient Greeks as a special virtue and was exalted by poets and philosophers.

The programme of the Olympic Games included 4 kinds of running events:

1. <u>The **Stadion**</u>. It was named after the place in which it was held. It was a straight race, from one end of the track to the other. Its length, which had been fixed at 600 feet, varied however, due to the difference in foot size from city to city. At Olympia it was 192.27m, in Athens 184.96m, in Epidaurus 181.30m, in Delphi 177.55m, in Pergamon 210m. The stadium at Olympia was the longest on the mainland of Greece and the one at Pergamon the longest in the Greek territories. The difference in length that the athletes had to cover in the different stadiums was of no importance because in antiquity the time did not count and the records were not registered. This length of 600 feet was the distance between the starting and finishing lines. The total length of the stadium was greater because it also included the necessary space for athletes to come to a halt after the finish. This supplementary space was 10.5m on the western end of the stadium at Olympia and 9.5m on the eastern side. The word **stadion**, besides

Runners of a sprint (Paris, the Louvre).

the event itself also meant the distance of 600 feet and was used as a measurement throughout antiquity.

The **stadion** was the oldest event of the Olympic Games and the only one for 13 Olympiads. From 632 BC (the 37th Olympiad) the **stadion** was held not only for men but also for children. Apart from being an event in its own right, the **stadion** was also included in the **pentathlon**.

2. <u>The **diaulos.**</u> This was also a sprint race but of two lengths of the **stadion**, that is 1,200 feet or 384.54m. It was the second oldest event, since it was introduced in 724 BC (the 14th Olympiad). Since in antiquity the athletes did not run around the stadium as they do today, but from one end to the other and back, the starting line of the **diaulos** was the finishing line of the single length race, so that the finish would remain the same and the runners would have the necessary space to come to a halt. At Olympia the start and the finish were on the western side of the stadium.

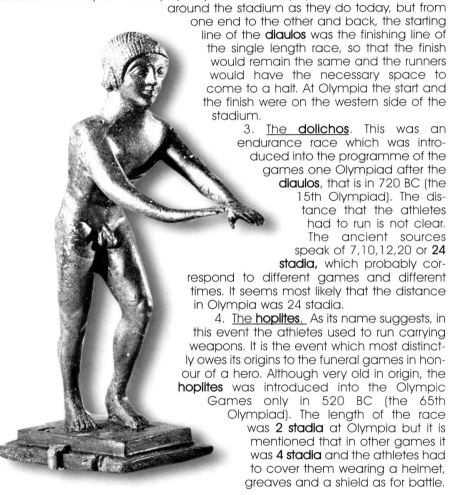

3. <u>The **dolichos.**</u> This was an endurance race which was introduced into the programme of the games one Olympiad after the **diaulos**, that is in 720 BC (the 15th Olympiad). The distance that the athletes had to run is not clear. The ancient sources speak of 7,10,12,20 or **24 stadia,** which probably correspond to different games and different times. It seems most likely that the distance in Olympia was 24 stadia.

4. <u>The **hoplites.**</u> As its name suggests, in this event the athletes used to run carrying weapons. It is the event which most distinctly owes its origins to the funeral games in honour of a hero. Although very old in origin, the **hoplites** was introduced into the Olympic Games only in 520 BC (the 65th Olympiad). The length of the race was **2 stadia** at Olympia but it is mentioned that in other games it was **4 stadia** and the athletes had to cover them wearing a helmet, greaves and a shield as for battle.

Bronze statuette of a runner. He is depicted about to start (Olympia, Archaeological Museum).

In the middle of the 5th century BC the greaves were abolished and later, after the 4th century BC so was the helmet, but the shield, wooden with a bronze plate, remained as long as the contest existed.

It is not clear if the athletes used their own weapons in the games. The variety of helmets and shields depicted in art shows that they used them at least during training. Pausanias mentions that in the temple of Zeus there were 24 shields which they used during this event. Furthermore, in an inscription that has been found in Delphi it reads that a certain Eudoxus donated the 10 shields for the 10 athletes who would be lined up at the start in the stadium.

The rarity of immortalization of the victorious **hoplites** runners in statues or in victory odes has led many experts to the conclusion that this contest was not especially popular but its continuous presence in the programme of the games till their abolishment, does not support such an opinion. Besides, its spectacular nature made it a beloved subject of the painters of vases.

The **hoplites** was the contest that closed every Olympiad, a fact that was considered to be a sign that the Truce was almost over.

Runners of a long distance course. The body is in upright position, the arms do not dangle and the stride is smaller than the one of the sprinters (London, British Museum).

The track

The place necessary for the track races to take place was nothing but a flat rectangular area, long enough so that the runners could reach top speed and wide enough so that several athletes could be lined up at the same time. This was ordained to be 600 feet long (600 X 0.32045 = 192.27m) and was called **stadion**.

For a long time, till the end of the 6th century BC, there were no real athletic installations at Olympia. The games, which were still of a small number, were held in a section of the sanctuary, close to the temple of Zeus and the spectators would watch them from the slopes of the hill Kronion. As time passed and the number of the spectators increased, the need for a real stadium became obvious. Such a construction, known today as "stadium I" was built around 560 BC. It was located next to the temple of Zeus, orientated E-W, that is parallel to the today's stadium and extended to within 80m of today's finish. It was of classical dimensions and on the northern side of the track there was a slope with a slight incline for the spectators. This stadium, at the end of the 6th century BC was replaced by another one, the "stadium II", the southern part of

which, designed for the spectators, was enclosed by a 3m high raised terrace, while the narrow western part was, like in its predecessor, open towards the sanctuary. This is the characteristic that differentiated the first two stadiums from the next one, "stadium III" of the middle of the 4th century BC, which can be seen today. Although it has the same SW-NE orientation as the previous ones, it is another 12m to the north and 75m to the east, that is, it is now located outside the **Altis**. This removal of the stadium from the sacred area, ostensibly for

An oplites runner. He carries the shield, the helmet and the greaves (Paris, the Louvre).

the necessary enlargement of the sanctuary, signals the political emancipation of the games and the gaining of a certain autonomy from the priesthood.

As in all the stadiums, at Olympia too, the embankments originally had no seats and the spectators would sit on the ground. But while in the other stadiums, possibly due to the influence of the architecture of the theatres, they started building seats, at Olympia the original model was kept till the end of antiquity. An exception was the seat of the priestess of Demeter Chamyne, on the northern side of the stadium and the **exedra** (podium) with the seats of the **Hellanodikai** and some officials, on the southern side.

For 'stadium III' embankments were built all around the track except on the northern side, where they exploited the natural slope of the hill Kronion. Shortly after the construction of the stadium they were raised another 3m and as a result the stadium finally had a capacity of 45.000 spectators. The existing so-called **Krypte** (hidden) entrance to the stadium was built in the Hellenistic period. It was a roofed corridor, along which there was a built-in seat for the waiting athletes. It was through this entrance that the **Hellanodikai** and the contestants entered the stadium, while for the spectators there were covered entrances under the embankments on all sides of the stadium.

The track of the stadium was a rectangular area, 212m long and 28.6m wide at the ends and up to 30,7m wide in the middle. The ground was a mixture of earth and sand. The area was surrounded by a stone draining channel which at regular intervals ran into square basins supplied by an underground system, from which both the athletes and the spectators drew up drinking water.

The distance that the athletes had to run was marked by two lines, exactly

Oplites runners (Naples, Archaeological Museum).

600 feet from each other. Originally these lines were simply scratched on the ground but as there was the risk that they would be moved, in the 5th century BC they were made permanent and were called **balbides**. They consisted of a series of oblong stone slabs, 0,45m wide, which had two parallel grooves 0,18m apart along their length where the athletes used to put their feet before the start. Along this series of slabs there were holes, 1.25m apart where poles were placed to separate the runners. Attached to these poles were horizontal moveable planks which prevented the athletes from starting too hastily. These planks were connected by strings held by the starter, who was standing behind and in the middle of the starting line. When the starter let go of all the strings holding the horizontal planks, they all fell together, permitting the athletes all to start at the same time.

The start

Our information about the way the races started is very restricted but taking into consideration the nature of the starting system, where the horizontal plank was at about breast height and also the depiction of such scenes in ancient art, we come to the conclusion that the method of starting was different from today's. The athletes started in an upright position, having one foot slightly in front of the other, the body slightly inclining forward and the knees bent, while the hands were outstretched, almost horizontal. The athletes were called to the **balbis** by the herald, were lined up in the lane which had been decided by the drawing of lots started with a certain signal given by the trumpeter or the starter.

The turn

In contrast to modern stadiums, the ancient ones had no bends to facilitate the turn. Of course this problem did not exist in the **stadion** event, during which the athletes had to run the length of the track only once. But in the other events this problem had to be faced. In the ancient sources the **kampter** (a post or small column) is mentioned as the turning point, as it is depicted in the vase paintings. It is, however, uncertain how the turn was affected. Formerly it had been claimed that all the athletes turned around the same **kampter**, something that does not seem probable, not only because it would not be practical but also because it would be unfair to those running in the outside lanes who would have to cover a longer distance. According to another opinion, each runner would run in his own lane and made a half-turn as soon as he reached the opposite **balbis**. They may have turned around the post and ran back in the corresponding next-door lane, which, however, would have caused collisions with any slower, oncoming runners. It seems most likely that in these events each runner had the exclusive use of two lanes, one for each direction. This theory also explains an inscription found in Delphi, which mentions the donation of ten shields for the **hoplites** course, while the stadium certainly had more lanes. Thus it seems obvious that only ten athletes could take part in the race at the same time. This is also what the word for the course, **diaulos** means "double flute" or "double channel" and it probably refers to the pairs of lanes for every athlete in this event.

The lanes were marked on the ground of the stadium with white powder, as shown in an inscription reporting the bequest of money for the purchase of this material.

The jump

The jump, as well as the foot-race, is one of the simplest events and stems from the natural attempt of man to jump over a natural obstacle. It is therefore peculiar that it does not seem to have enjoyed from the beginning the popularity that the other events did in the eyes of the ancient Greeks. It is mentioned only once by Homer, in the Odyssey as being held on the island of the Phaiakes, while in the Iliad it is not even included in the games in honour of Patroclus. Pindar does not attribute a prehistoric origin to this event, as it is not mentioned among the five games that Hercules introduced at Olympia. This leads us to the conclusion that the jump was never an event of its own, but always constituted a part of the **pentathlon**.

The jump that the athletes executed during the games was always a long jump. No doubt the ancient Greeks practiced other types of jump, for example a jump with the help of a pole, something similar to the modern pole vault, as we can see in illustrations on vases, but it can not have been so popular, as it was never included in the games.

The characteristic that differentiates the jump of those times from the modern one is the use of the **halteres**. They were weights made of stone or metal, which the athletes used to hold, one in each hand, and which they used to let fall in the sand pit shortly before landing. Their purpose was to improve the performance of the athletes, as mentioned by Aristotle and proved by modern experiments.

Athletes training in jumping. They are holding halteres of the type called makroi
(Boston, Museum of Fine Arts)

The simplest type of **halteres** was a solid piece of stone or metal, slightly indented, so that the athlete would be able to grip it. In the classical period there were two basic categories of **halteres**, the **makroi** (long) ones, which exercised the shoulders and the arms and the **sphairoeideis** (spherical) ones, which exercised the fingers too. There were also some others such as the **elleipsoeideis**, (elliptical), the **amphibareis**, the **amphisphairoi** etc. The weight of the **halteres** varied from 1.5 to 2 kg and was obviously proportionate to the physical build of the athletes. The much bigger **halteres** of up to 4.6 kg that have been found must have been votive pieces.

The use of the **halteres** was not compulsory but the athletes used to use them often because the boost that they gave to the jump was significant. Besides, they were not only used during the jumps but also during training in the gymnasiums, in order to develop their arm muscles, the way the modern athletes use weights.

Another characteristic of the jump in antiquity was that it was always performed to the music of a flute, so that the movements of the jumper would be rhythmical and harmonic. The ancient Greeks believed that the music constituted a necessary link between the spiritual and the physical and that it thus succeeds in creating not only good athletes but also mature free citizens, which was the goal of Greek societies of the classical period.

A riddle that has not yet been solved is exactly what kind of jump it was: a simple, double or a triple one. The question is raised because of the information about distances, which could have been achieved only if the jump were a triple. It is mentioned, for example, that Phaullos from Kroton in south Italy jumped at the beginning of the 5th century BC, 16.28m and that the Spartan Chionis jumped 16.31m in 664 BC. It is a fact that the jump by Phaullos made such an impression on the people that the sentence " to jump over the sand pit " became a saying used throughout antiquity. But since the pit was 16m long it is impossible that he jumped over it with a simple jump. Of course another explanation might be that the admiration and the adoration of the ancient Greeks of the athletes was such that the real record was swelled and the length of 16m did not correspond to reality. Anyway, most of the experts today tend to agree on the conclusion that the jump of the ancient **pentathlon** was a triple jump.

It is not clear if the athletes used a run-up for their jumps. If so it would not have been a long one because the **halteres** would have been a definite hindrance. On a small amount of vases the athletes are depicted ready to jump from standing. It can not be ruled out that they made such a jump, which however, was not included in the programme of the games.

The place where the jumps took place was the sand pit, a rectangular dug area, 50 feet (16m) long, full of soft earth. On one side there was the **bater**, a firm take-off ramp, made of wood or stone, on which the athletes had to step before they jumped. The length of the jump was measured with the help of wooden sticks, the **kanones**, and the records were marked with small wooden pegs, that they used to stick in the ground, as is clearly visible on many vases. It is not known in which part of the stadium the pit was located but it certainly would not have been difficult to prepare such an area on the day of the event itself .

The discus throwing

Discus throwing was not held as an independent event either but it constituted part of the **pentathlon**. It seems that it was one of the oldest events, since Perseus, the founder of Mycenae, was regarded as its inventor. According to the legend, the king of Argos, Akrissios would not allow his daughter, Danae, to get married because, according to an oracle, he would be killed by her son. However the god Zeus, transformed himself into golden rain and entered the prison where she was being held and some months later she gave birth to Perseus, whom his grandfather then tried unsuccessfully to do away with. Many years later, during some funeral games in Argos, Perseus threw his disc and unwittingly killed Akrissios, thus verifying the oracle. The god Apollo too, had killed the young Yakinthos by accident with his discus and the same thing happened to other mythological heroes. Ulysses too, took part in the discus throwing on the island of the Phaiakes and other Greeks in the funeral games of Patroclus.

The discus was originally a heavy object, made of stone or metal, which had to be thrown as far as possible. This object, in the funeral games of Patroclus, was a solid, metallic mass, called by Homer **solos**, which was thrown with the help of a strap or rope, that was passed through it, as in the modern hammer throw. In the land of Phaiakes, on the other hand, it was made of stone, as were the discuses of the prehistoric heroes mentioned by Pindar. Perhaps up until the 6th century BC the stone discuses were used alongside the metallic ones, and then were replaced completely by them.

The discus in the classical period was made of iron, bronze or lead. It was, as it is today, round, bi-convex in section and ended in a wide circumference. It often had engraved illustrations of athletes, animals or geometrical designs. Odes and other inscriptions, for instance the treaty of the truce of Olympia would also be inscribed on the discuses.

The size and the weight of the discuses are still problematic. Archaeological research has brought to light discuses with diameters of 16 to 35 cm and weights of 1,3 to 6,4 kg. At Olympia itself, where there should have been two sizes of discus, one for the men and one for the boys, discuses have been found with seven different dimensions and weights. It is most probable that they used different discuses at different periods of time. Anyway during the games competitors would throw the same discus, because otherwise it would not have been possible to

Bronze discus with votive inscription. (Olympia, Archaeological Museum).

determine the winner fairly. Pausanias alludes to this when he writes that three discuses were kept in the treasury of the Sikyonians which were for use in the **pentathlon**.

From illustrations in art but also from a narration by Philostratos it is to be supposed that the throw of the discus was performed more or less the same way as it is today. First the discus thrower raised the discus with both hands over the head and then he lowered it with the right hand, turning the trunk slightly to the right. The weight of the body fell on the right leg, which was behind, while the left one was stretched forward. He made some preliminary swings and then lowered the body, bent the knees even more, before fully extending, the right hand holding the discus downwards and backwards, and then by suddenly straightening knees and moving the weight onto the front left leg, he threw the discus forwards and upwards. It is not known if, before the throw, they made use of some kind of run-up or rotation, as is done today. The **balbis** from which they threw the discus was not circular, like the modern ones, but rectangular and open on one side, from which the athlete entered. It was narrow, wide enough only for one person. We do not know if the athlete was allowed to use the unlimited space on the open side of the rectangular, which in any case would not have helped, as what is important is the rotation and not the forward thrust The restricted area of the **balbis**, the lines of which they were not allowed to step on, limited the athletes to throwing the discus along the central axis of the stadium, thus preventing possible accidents. Despite the fact that the stadiums in antiquity were narrower than the modern ones, no cases of injury during the games, either of an athlete or of a spectator, were reported.

The throws of the athletes were marked with the **semata**, wooden pegs, like those used to mark the jumps and were measured with wooden poles. The athletes had the right of five throws, of which the best one counted. We know almost nothing about the distance of the throws. It is mentioned that Phaullus threw the discus a distance of 95 feet (30.4m) but we can not evaluate the throw as we do not know the weight of the discus he threw.

....

The discus thrower by Myron. One of the most famous statues of athletes. Roman copy (Rome, Museo Nayionale Romano).

The javelin throw

Together with the jump and the discus it is the third and last contest which is not to be found in the games as an independent event but constituted part of the **pentathlon**. Its obvious relation to hunting and war explains its long history and its presence in the legends. According to Pindar, it was one of the events of the games that were held for the first time at Olympia by Hercules. In the Iliad it is mentioned as an event in the funeral games of Patroclus and also as a way in which the soldiers of Achilles used to pass their time. In the Odyssey too, the suitors of Penelope used to amuse themselves by throwing the discus and the javelin.

In antiquity there were two kinds of javelin throws, the **ekebolos** and the **estochastikos**. The aim of the first one, which also was the most popular, was to throw the javelin as far as possible. The second kind, on the other hand, aimed at hitting a fixed target and had more practical importance, as it trained the young men in using the javelin as a weapon in battle.

Apart from the two kinds of throws there were in ancient Greece two types of javelin, too: those which were a simple pole, sharpened at one end, as long as the height of a man and lighter than the javelin of the warriors- as suggest-

Depiction of a javelin thrower (Berlin, Staatliche Museen).

ed by its name **apotomas**, which means " of reduced dimensions"- and those which were equipped with a metallic head. For the **estochastikos** throw the second type of javelin would have been necessary in order to stick into the target. But for the **ekebolos** too, at least during the games they must have used a sharp javelin with a metallic head, since the throw was valid only when the javelin stuck in the ground and the measurement of the throw was possible. In ancient art, where we often see javelins without a head, they obviously depict scenes of the gymnasium, where they would use such javelins in order to prevent accidents. Such javelins with a rounded tip were suggested for safety reasons, by Xenophon for the training of the soldiers. The head of the athletic javelin probably caused the death of a young man by a fellow athlete, whom the Athenian orator Antiphon defended in a speech. The unfortunate athlete had accidentally passed in front of the target in the gymnasium.

The presence of a metallic head at the end of the javelin moved its central weight and the throw on the one hand lost in distance but on the other hand gained in stability. For this reason, in cases when the javelin had no head, they attached an iron ring to the end which had the same practical effect.

The only difference between the ancient and the modern javelin throw was the use of the **ankyle**, that is of a leather thong, 30 to 40 cm long, which was wound tightly around the middle of the javelin, at its central weight was. A loop, 6 to 10 cm in this thong through which they passed the forefinger or the forefinger along with the middle finger. Before the throw, the athlete pushed the javelin backward with the left hand in order to stretch the **ankyle** and to tighten the fingers of the right hand that were passed through it. Then, after a run-up, he threw the javelin the way modern athletes do. There is also a theory that the **ankyle** was bound in such a way that it remained in the athlete's hand after the throw. The javelins of the warriors and the hunters were also supplied with **ankyles** but they were permanently fixed, while in the athletic ones the contestant bound them the way he preferred. It is a fact that the **ankyle** increased the

Fragment of a vase depicting a discus thrower (Würzburg, Martin von Wagner Museum)

throwing power because it stabilized the grip and consequently it increased the distance that the javelin could cover. Experiments made by the soldiers of Napoleon the Great proved that the length of the throw can, with the help of the **ankyle**, even be doubled. In any case the throws of the ancient Greeks cannot be estimated since the weight of the javelins is not known.

As in the case of the discus throw, the place from which the throws were made was the **balbis**, which had the form of a rectangle, open on the one side. It is possible that they used the same **balbis** which was used for the discus throw and that its front line was the finishing line of the races, judging from the name **terma** (finish) by which it is called by Pindar.

In order for a throw to be valid the javelin had not only to stick in the ground but also to fall in a marked off area of the stadium. The distances, as in the other throws, were marked with wooden pegs and measured with the **kanones**.

The other kind of javelin throw, the **estochastikos**, was usually performed on horseback and was not included in the Olympic Games.

Estochastikos javelin throwing. It was usually performed by riding athletes and was not included in the programme of the games (London , British Museum).

The wrestling

Pale (wrestling) is the oldest and most widespread sport in the whole world, because it constitutes the first example of unarmed combat. The scenes of wrestling depicting the best known Greek heroes such as Hercules and Theseus against their savage adversaries, were the most eloquent way of depicting the struggle of civilization and spirit against barbarity. And it is no coincidence that the words relating to this contest such as **pale, paleuein** mean generally fight or struggle.

According to one legend, wrestling was invented by Palaistra, daughter of the god Hermes, thus bringing great joy to the whole earth. According to another, Theseus invented it when wrestling against Kerkyon, and to another it was the goddess Athena, who also invented the regulations of the contest.

In mythology we can find a large number of heroes who took part in wrestling matches, but the first detailed description is made by Homer in the Iliad, when he narrates at length how Ulysses defeated Ajax. Apart from the popularity that wrestling enjoyed among ordinary people, it was greatly appreciated by the celebrities of antiquity. Plato, for example, in the " Laws" declares that wrestling develops all parts of the body, giving it the desired strength and beauty, and Plutarch attributes the victory of the Thebans over the Spartans in the battle of Leuktra to their ability to wrestle and calls it "the cleverest and most technical of the contests " , while some others go so far as to regard wrestling as the combination of an art form and a science.

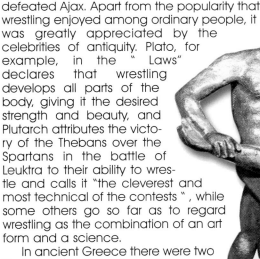

In ancient Greece there were two kinds of wrestling, the **orthia pale** (standing wrestling) and the **kato pale** (wrestling on the ground). The aim of the first one was simply to throw your opponent onto the ground, while the second one continued on the ground

Bronze complex of wrestlers (Munich, Antikensammlungen).

The initial position of a pair of wrestlers (Athens, National Archaeological Museum)

until one of the wrestlers conceded defeat. The standing wrestling was the most popular version of the contest and this is why it was the one included in the programme of the games, as a part of the **pentathlon** as well as an independent event. The **kato pale** was similar to the **pankration** in that the adversaries continued the fight on the ground but it differed in that striking the other was prohibited and each athlete simply applied holds on his opponent.

Lots were drawn to decide the pairings. Lucian (Hermot. 39) informs us about the way that the procedure was carried out. The **Hellanodikai** put small pieces of wood, the size of a bean, on which a letter was inscribed, into a silver receptacle. There were as many lots as athletes. Before drawing his lot every athlete came in front of the table, where the receptacle was placed, and said a short prayer to Zeus. Those athletes who had drawn the same letter had to fight against each other. They were a minimum of five and maximum of eight pairs of athletes chosen. If the number of the participants was odd, one athlete had a bye to the next round without having fought and in this case he was called **ephedros**. This gave him a definite advantage over his adversaries, whom he faced in the next round without being tired. This is why many athletes, in commemorative inscriptions, made a special mention of the fact that they had won the **kotinos anephedroi,** that is without a bye in any of the rounds of the contest. It seems that, as happened in all the physically demanding events, there were no official breaks during the contest. However, sometimes it happened that an athlete asked for a short interruption in order to catch his breath or take care of his injuries.

As we can see depicted in art, the initial pose of the athletes was similar to the modern one; that is, with the legs apart and knees bent, the bodies and the heads leaning forward slightly, like two animals poised to attack. There were a variety of holds and the tricks used which had different names. Neck holds, holding from the waist and squeezing one's adversary tightly with both arms, lifting one's adversary in the air and throwing him to the ground and many grips of the hands and the wrists were the most common. According to Pausanias, Leontiskos from Messina in Sicily, who won at Olympia in 456 and 452 BC used a hand grip and managed to break his opponent's fingers. These methods were obviously not prohibited, but were, however, disapproved of by the spectators, as Philostratus clearly says in his work " Eikones".

The wrestlers used to fight with their bodies covered with oil and dust. The smearing on of oil was very healthy because it prevented the sand and the dust of the arena from entering the pores of the skin, and the dust that they used to put on their oiled bodies prevented the hands of the athletes from slipping when they tried several grips. This layer of oil and dust was removed at the end of the contest with the **stlegis**, an oblong iron or bronze tool, curved at the one end. The **stlegis** was an indispensable accessory to the athletes, a fact which explains the frequency of its depiction in art as well as its presence in the tombs of young men.

In order for somebody to be declared the winner in the standing wrestling, he had either to throw his opponent onto the ground three times or to make him **apagoreuein** (concede). A fall was counted as the touching of the ground of any part of the body. If both athletes fell at the same time, the fall did not count. The athlete had the right to concede defeat on the grounds of exhaustion. In this case he had to raise the forefinger or the forefinger and the middle finger of the right hand and he **apagoreuein**.

In one case a victory **akoniti** is mentioned in the wrestling. This expression means "without dust"; that is without the athlete applying the necessary dust before the contest, and concerns some very rare cases in the heavy contests when a very strong athlete had no opponent for the event. Milon from Kroton in south Italy won in this way.

If the contest remained undecided or neither wrestler had managed to throw his adversary three times, the wreath was offered to Zeus.

As in all the games, wrestling too, had its regulations which had to be respected by the athletes. Punching, grips on the genitals, biting and fighting out of bounds were all prohibited. When the wrestlers moved out of the prescribed area, the judges interrupted the fight, which then resumed with the same hold or position that they had before the interruption. Holding the legs was probably also banned but they were allowed to use their legs to trip their opponent and thus throw him onto the ground.

Although wrestling was undoubtedly a painful contest, only one fatal accident is mentioned, in 484 BC (the 74th Olympiad), when a wrestler, on jumping, broke his neck.

The arena where the **orthia pale** was held was the **skamma** (sand pit), a square area, which, as its name shows was dug and then filled with a layer of sand. The second kind of wrestling was performed in an area where the ground was watered so much that it became like mud.

The pentathlon

As its name suggests, the **pentathlon** was a composite game, consisting of five other events; the **stadion** (sprint race), the jump, the discus throw, the javelin throw and the wrestling. It was considered by the ancient Greeks as the most perfect event because it developed all parts of the body equally, thus endowing the pentathlete with physical beauty, harmony and health. Such an opinion is stated by the philosopher Aristotle (Rhetor. 1361b) and also by the famous doctor of antiquity Galen (3.2).

Because of its composite nature, the **pentathlon** must have been invented in the historic period. Even though Philostratos mentions it as a prehistoric contest, Homer does not know of it and he mentions the five events as independent, a fact that is verified by Pindar (Isthm. 1.26). It was introduced into the Olympic Games in 708 BC (the 18th Olympiad) and was also held once for children, in 628 BC (the 38th Olympiad).

Determining what the programme of the **pentathlon** was is difficult, as far as the order of events and how the winner was determined are concerned. The fact that the last event was the wrestling makes that event without doubt of decisive importance. From what Pindar (II Isthm.) mentions we can presume an order of discus, javelin and wrestling and, from an epigram for the famous pentathlete Phaullus, we can suppose that the jump preceded the discus. Therefore the order may have been: **stadion**, jump, discus, javelin wrestling.

There is no concordance of opinion about how the winner was determined. It would be impractical to believe that the same athlete would have been able to win all five contests. Maybe a victory in at least three events, of which one would certainly be the wrestling, was enough. This theory would also explain the term **triakter** mentioned by Pausanias.

Athletes of the pentathlon. A jumper with the halteres, two javelin throwers and a discus thrower (London, British Museum).

The boxing (pugilism)

Boxing is one of the events which has roots that undoubtedly go back to Greek prehistory. Archaeological findings make it clear that it held a special position in the preference of the inhabitants of Crete and the Cyclades, where the athletes used to wear not only gloves but also protective helmets, in order to avoid punches to the head. On the mainland of Greece, boxing is mentioned for the first time by Homer in the Iliad, where Epeus defeated Euryalus, and in the Odyssey in the games that the Phaiakes organized on their island.

In mythology , several gods and heroes are mentioned as the inventors of the contest, like Hercules, Theseus and also Apollo, who was also the protector or patron of the sport. Nevertheless, despite its long history, boxing was introduced into the Olympic Games only in 688 BC(the 23rd Olympiad). The first winner was Onomastos from Smyrne in Asia Minor, who also invented the rules of the sport.

Bronze statue of a boxer with oxeis himantes (Rome, Museo Nazionale Romano).

Homer mentions that the boxers covered their hands with straps of thin ox leather that protected the joints of the fingers and the wrist but that also made the punches less painful when hit. These **himantes** (boxing straps), which were called **himantes malakoteroi** (soft straps), were 3 to 3,50 m in length. They were wound several times around the four fingers, leaving the thumb uncovered, and passed diagonally across the palm and the upper part of the hand, tied around the wrist or up to the middle of the forearm (Paus. 8.40.3, Philostr. Gymn. 10, Plut. Eth. 80). These soft **himantes** were in use till the end of the 5th century BC, when they were replaced by another kind, which protected the hand more efficiently and which, because of their shape, were called **sphaires** (globes). They were reinforced at the first joint of the fingers, externally with straps of harder leather and internally with wool (Plat.

Boxers with himantes of the type called sphairai (London, British Museum).

Laws 83o, Plut. Eth. 825).

At about the end of the 4th century BC this type of **himantes** was replaced by a new one, the **oxeis** (sharp). They were no longer straps that the athletes would have to tie and untie every time they had to fight but real boxing gloves, which they put on before the match. They were further reinforced at the joints of the fingers with hard leather, as their name indicates, which made the punches stronger and more painful. They also left the finger tips free and extended to the middle of the forearm, where there was a thick band of wool, which either protected the forearm from knocks or was used by the athletes in order to wipe the sweat from their eyes, in the way the tennis players of today do. These **himantes** were in use in Greece till the end of the 2nd century BC. In Roman times, in order for the contest to become more aggressive, in other words more enjoyable for the spectators who now wanted to see blood in the various spectacles, the **caestus** was invented, which were boxing gloves reinforced with iron or lead and often had nails at the joints of the fingers - clearly a Roman idea!

By following the development in the form of the **himantes** we can not only see the changes in the technique of this sport but also out line the development of athletics in general, and by extension, that of ancient Greek society throughout the centuries. In the oldest description of boxing, by Homer, Epeus defeats his opponent with a strong punch to the face and knocks him down, but immediately afterwards he hurries to pull him up, showing clearly his sportsmanship. At the time when the **himantes** were still soft, boxing demanded agility, skillfulness, and intelligence. In short, it was an art form. With the introduction of the **oxeis himantes**, the punches became more powerful, the fight became more defensive, more physical and less technical and much more violent. The stout build of the athletes counted more than their intelligence. A typical case is the one mentioned by Dion Chryssostomos (Rhet. 29), of the boxer Melancomas, who managed to avoid his opponents' punches for two days, till they, exhausted, conceded defeat. It was already a time in which the event had become popularized and the masses had become alienated from the ideals of the mythological heroes, and demanded more violence rather than fair play.

Of course, the heavier the gloves of the boxers became, the more frequent the accidents were. What's more these were sometimes even fatal. Injuries that caused permanent disfigurement to the face of the boxers, especially the nose, the teeth and the ears were ,however, more common, and as a consequence, these athletes sometimes became the subject of ridicule by the satirical poets. One such poet, Lucilius, (c 60 AD), wrote about the boxer Stratophon: " when Ulysses arrived home after twenty years, his dog, Argos recognized him at once. But you, after four hours of boxing, have become unrecognizable not only to the dogs but also to the city and if you look at yourself in the mirror, you will cry out swearing: This is not me, Stratophon". The same poet wrote about Olympikos: " don't you ever look at yourself reflected in the water because you will die like Narcissus, but for quite the opposite reason" (Anthologia Pal. 11.75,76). As you will know, Narcissus died of astonishment at his own beauty on seeing his face reflected in the water.

The training of the boxers was almost the same as it is today. The athletes always wore the so-called **epotides**, that is protective covers of leather or metal on the ears, which they had to take off before the contest. Sometimes they trained by fighting holding onto each other only by the fingertips, an exercise known as **akrocheiriasmos** (Arist. Nik. Eth.3.1). When there was no opponent to train with, athletes did a kind of exercise as if there someone facing them, which was called **skiamachia** (shadow fighting) (Plat. Laws 8. 830, Paus. 6.10.3, Plut. Eth. 130, Dion Chryssost. 32-44). On other occasions they used the **koryx**, a punch bag hung at shoulder height and filled with sand or other lighter substances. They used to practice various punches on the **koryx**, exactly like modern boxers.

The athletes of the heavy events also trained by weight-lifting, which was known to the ancient Greeks but it was never an event in its own right. In Olympia a 143.50 kg stone has been found, which, according to the inscription on it, the athlete Bybon is proud to have lifted over his head with one hand.

Although the training of the ancient boxers was similar to that of the modern ones, the contest itself was rather different. In antiquity the contest did not take place in a roped off area which would have restricted the movements of the athletes and would have helped the one throw decisive punches to the other. There was also no time limit within which the contest should finish. Victory was acknowledged when the one boxer fell unconscious to the ground or when he as in the wrestling, conceded defeat by raising his hand with one or two fingers. If, by the end of the day, there was no winner, the judges could apply the **klimax**; that is a system according to which each athlete in turn received a punch from his adversary, without trying to avoid it. The winner was the one who endured the most punches. The order was fixed by lots because the one who punched first had a very clear advantage. The **klimax** was a very tough solution and it seems that it was used only in exceptional cases. During the contests there were no regular breaks, as in the modern rounds, although it is mentioned that the judge had the right, if both athletes agreed, to interrupt the contest for a while, in order for them to regain their strength or take care of their injuries.

It is noteworthy that, although the athletes were classified into categories according to their age there was no classification according to weight. Considering that the pairs of athletes were chosen with the drawing of lots, it stood to reason that the heavier athletes had a much better chance of winning, and as a consequence, in the passage of time, they dominated the event and thus it became slower and less technical.

From the boxing depicted in art we observe that the athletes used both hands. The general posture of the body was more erect than it is today and the punches were usually direct. The opinion that they preferred to hit the opponent on the head, rather than the body, does not seem to be supported by archaeological findings. The footwork of the boxers were very agile and they deliberately tried to maneuver their opponent to face the sun so that he could not see their moves so well.

There cannot have been many rules and regulations for the boxing. Holding your opponent was prohibited as were punches to the genitals and biting. The boxing **himantes** too had to be made according to the regulations and this is why they were checked before the beginning of the contest. They were not allowed to have more than the regulation leather reinforcement or to be made of pig skin.

Head of a boxer. Fragment of a statue from Olympia. The nose has the characteristic deformation of these athletes (Athens, National Archaeological Museum).

The pankration

The **pankration** was a combination of wrestling and boxing, or as it is exactly mentioned by the commentator of Plato (The Republ. 1,338), a combination of incomplete wrestling and incomplete boxing. It is not mentioned at all by Homer and it appears in the Olympic Games in 648 BC (the 33rd Olympiad). It was a particularly popular event, the winners of which were praised by great poets. Pindar wrote eight victory odes to **pankratiastes** and Philostratus, in his description of the event (Eikon. 2.6), calls it the most appropriate one for men. The prestige it had is shown by the epithet **pankrates**, which was attributed to the father of the gods, Zeus, but also to the strongest of the Greek heroes, Hercules.

Although the **pankration** combined wrestling with boxing, it also had some elements that are not to be found in either of these. The athletes did not wear boxing gloves and consequently could hit the adversary with the fist as well as with the open palm. In contrast to the boxing, blows with the legs to all parts of the body were allowed. They were generally allowed to use all the holds of the wrestling and all the punches of the boxing and it was only biting and gouging the eyes, mouth or nose, and using the nails which were prohibited. These prohibitions

A pankration contest. One athlete has put his hand in his adversary's eye and the judge is about to interrupt the game (London, British Museum).

55

did not apply during the training of the athletes in Sparta, where the **pankration** was considered as preparation for war. In relation to this there is the episode with Alcibiades (Plut. Alcib. 2), who had trained in Sparta and who, when fighting in the **pankration** in a gymnasium of Athens and being afraid that he would be defeated, bit his adversary. He shouted at him contemptuously: "Alcibiades, you bite like the women" and the always quick-witted Alcibiades answered: "no, I bite like the lions".

There were two kinds of **pankration**, the **ano** (upper) **pankration**, and the **kato** (low) **pankration**. In the first one the athletes tried to throw their opponent onto the ground, while in the second, one athlete fell onto the other trying to immobilize him and force him to surrender. In the games they used to fight only in the **kato pankration**, while the **ano pankration**, being less physical, was used only in training.

During the contest the athletes had, besides their strength, to use their intelligence too, and there were some tricks that were often used. One of them was the **hyptiasmos**, that is where the athlete would fall to the ground on his back,

Grip from the legs in a pankration game (New York, Metropolitan Museum).

not simply to avoid falling on his chest in order not to leave his back and his neck unprotected but deliberately, in order to be able to use his legs and arms to strike some decisive blows to the stomach of his opponent, in case he tried to fall on him, or even to grasp his opponent's head with his legs. Pindar, in his ode to the **pankratiastes** Melissos from Thebes who won in the Isthmian Games, compares this very aptly with the way that the fox falls on its back when the eagle is ready to attack her (Pind. Isthm. 3.76).

When an athlete fell front first to the ground, his opponent would apply a very dangerous grip, the **klimakismos**; that is, he fell on him, immobilized him by locking his legs around his waist and applied, with terrible strength, a hold to his neck. Such a hold often meant the end of the contest, because the adversary usually gave in rather than risk choking. Just how dangerous the **klimakismos** was becomes clear from the episode concerning Arrachion, mentioned by Pausanias (8.40.2) and by Philostratus (Eikon. 2.6), who, under the pressure of such a hold, grasped his adversary's foot and dislocated his anklebone. The latter, because of the pain, conceded but it was too late for Arrachion, who expired shortly afterwards. Nevertheless the judges declared him the winner, not because he died but because his adversary had conceded defeat and later his hometown, Figalia in Arcadia, erected a statue to him.

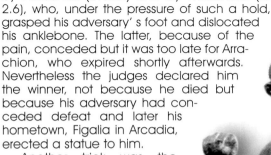

Another trick was the **apopternisein** where one athlete grasped the foot of the other from by heel so he would lose his balance. A kick to the stomach (**gastrisein**) was also common.

The fact that such tricks were allowed is borne out by drawing on vases, by the texts of ancient writers like Aristophanes (Hipp. 272, 454) and Lucian (Anach. 9). In a description by the latter, we read that despite the bloody knocks, the judge, not only does not stop the contest but actively encourages the fighters to continue.

Despite the violent nature of the event and the frequent injuries, the cases of serious accidents to the **pankratiastes** were fewer than those of the boxers, because in the **pankration** it was not the head that was the main target, and besides that, the athletes did not wear **himantes** and the blows were not so powerful. Consequently, facially, the **pankratiastes** did not have the characteristic appearance of the boxers. Less facially disfigured and also less corpulent, they had, according to Philostratos (Gymnast. 36) to be strong and agile in order to turn easily, light, fast and wily in order to take up all the positions but also to avoid the knocks.

An athlete admits his defeat (apagoreuein) (London, British Museum).

The equestrian events

*T*hese races and especially the chariot races, were the pre-eminently aristocratic events of ancient Greece. They already had this privileged character in the Mycenean period, as is clearly implied by the description of the funeral games of Patroclus in the Iliad, and they kept it throughout the classical period, till the end of antiquity. This phenomenon is explained by the fact that only a certain social class could afford the maintenance of horses, chariots and at the same time pay the charioteers who, from the historic period on, were not usually the owners of the horses. The races thus became the way par excellence in which every kind of privileged people, **tyrants**, kings and members of famous families increased their prestige, and the racecourse became the place in which to demonstrate one's wealth and political power.

The origin of these games goes back, of course, to the mythological period, and their patron was the god Poseidon, to whom the epithet **hippios** was also attributed. The importance that the chariot races had in the minds of the Greeks becomes clear also from one of the basic legends of the sanctuary of Olympia, according to which, as has been already mentioned, Pelops won a chariot race and then dominated the whole area. The long history of the events of the racecourse, as well as the numerous archaeological findings from the sanctuary, depicting chariots or riders, dating back to early periods, contradict the information of Pausanias that the first event of the racecourse, the chariot race, was introduced into the Olympic Games only in 680 BC (the 24th Olympiad).

There are few ancient texts to enlighten us about the equestrian events and the place where they were held, but the most important are descriptions by Sophocles in "Electra" and by Pausanias (6.20.10-19). The archaeological findings are not at all helpful either, as no racecourse has been preserved in the whole Greek territory. The racecourse at Olympia has completely disappeared due to the flooding of the Alpheios. It was located to the north-east of the stadium and parallel to it. Originally and till the classical period, it was a flat area, long and wide enough for a large number of chariots to be able to line up and race. Later, an artificial embankment was built for the spectators on the northern side, up against the corresponding southern embankment of the stadium and another one on the southern side of the racecourse. Probably, as in the case of the stadium, there were no tiers of seats for the spectators, with the possible exception of some privileged seats for the judges and the officials. The western part of the racecourse was marked by the portico of Agnaptos, the form and the dimensions of which are not known. To the east there was another artificial embankment. There were entrances for the spectators on the east and on the south, under the embankments.

On the racecourse itself, along the long axis, there were two small pillars, the **nyssai**, about 400m apart, around which the chariots effected the turns. The western one also marked the start and the finish of the race. Between these two pillars there was a stone or wooden wall, the **embolon**, which was to prevent head-on collisions between the chariots. A compete circuit, an **hippios**, was about 780m that is four **stadions**. The width of the racecourse at Olympia must have been about 200m that is about one **stadion**, so that many chariots could be lined up. In the famous games that took place in Delphi in 462 BC, 41 chariots started, of which only the one of the king of Cyrene, Arkesilus finished and it is possible that the racecourse at Olympia was even bigger. It is worth mentioning two exceptional racecourses, the ones of Athens and of Delos, that were so long (the one in Athens was 8 **stadions** long, the length of other one is not known), that the participating chariots did not always have to turn but simply starting from the one end they finished at the other. These racecourses were called **akampioi** (without turning point).

The most impressive part of the Greek racecourse was certainly the start. The detailed description by Pausanias gives us a clear idea of this really interesting conception. The start was constructed in such a way that it looked like a triangle, " like the prow of a ship ", the ram of which pointed towards the racecourse and the open end towards the portico of Agnaptos. The prow was supposed to form an angle of 60o and its ram was not in exactly in line with the long axis of the racecourse but a little to the south, so that after the horses started, they would more easily be able to converge on a specific point of the southern part of the racecourse, where the proper race would start. A bronze dolphin was placed more or less at the end of the ram. Along each of the long sides of the triangle, which were about 400 feet long, small stalls were constructed, open at the front, for the horses or the chariots that were allotted each to a specific stall after the drawing of lots. A rope was stretched across the front of the stalls as a kind of barrier. In about the middle of the triangle they constructed, for every Olympic Games, an altar of mud bricks, whitewashed on the outside, on which they put a bronze eagle with outstretched wings. At the start of the race, sounded by a trumpeter, the starter activated the special mechanism that was located under the altar and the eagle was raised so as to be visible to the spectators who were thus made aware of the start of the race, while simultaneously the dolphin began to be gradually lowered in synchronization with the opening of the stalls. When the ropes in front of the first horses fell they started galloping. As soon as they arrived level with those waiting, those ropes fell too and so on until all the horses were in a line, level with the ram of the prow, from which the real race started. From this point on, every rider did his best to reach the turning point first and to gain the inside lane of the racecourse, which was the shortest one.

This way of starting compensated for the inevitable injustice that would be done to those athletes who were in the outside lane of the racecourse if they all started in a straight line, or even a diagonal one. Since the basic difficulty was turning around the **nyssa**, the riders who had been picked to start on the left of the starting line would have been very much at a disadvantage. However, with this invention, the athletes who started from further back would overcome this handicap by arriving at a gallop at the point from which the others who were in front of them would start.

Another advantage of this method of starting off was that, with the system of the ropes, the danger of a false start was eliminated. Finally, we should not overlook the undoubtedly aesthetic effect of this complicated invention, with the sound of the trumpets that gave the signal, the moving metallic animals, the staggered start of the horses and all this in front of a delirious crowd that were enthusiastically cheering on the riders while at the same time admiring· the starting system itself.

The person who came up with this way of starting was a certain Kleoitas, sculptor from Athens, who was so proud of it, that on a statue of his in Athens he wrote the following epigram: " Made by Kleoitas, son of Aristocles, who first invented the way of starting off the horses in Olympia " (Paus. 6.20.14). An improvement to the mechanism must have been made later by a certain Aristides.

Apart from the constructions that were necessary for the running of the races there were also some others on the racecourse. On the northern side, opposite the finishing line, there was the podium of the **Hellanodikai**. At about the same height, in the middle of the racecourse close to one of the **nyssa**, probably stood the bronze statue of Hippodameia holding the winner's wreath, with which she was about to crown Pelops. Inside the triangular space formed by the starting stalls, towards the portico of Agnaptos, there were numerous altars, dedicated to various divinities: to Poseidon Hippios, Hera Hippia, Ares and Athena Hippioi and also to the Dioskouroi, the goddess Tyche (fortune), to Pan and to Aphrodite.

On the other side of the racecourse, close to the eastern **nyssa**, where the turning point of the horses was, there was another round altar, relating to a strange and as yet unexplained belief of the ancient Greeks. It was dedicated to **Taraxippos**, who, as his name indicates caused terror to horses. The ancient sources about this superstition are clear. Pausanias (6.20.15) informs us: " When the horses ran close to it (the altar), they were immediately overcome with fear for no obvious reason and because of this fear confusion ensued and the chariots were usually smashed and the charioteers injured. For this reason the riders make sacrifices in the hope that **Taraxippos** would be favorable to them".

What exactly **Taraxippos** was remains a mystery. According to one theory it was the tomb of some heroes, among whom a suitor of Hippodameia, whom her father, Oinomaos, killed or of Oinamaos's charioteer, Myrtilos, whom Pelops killed and then made sacrifices in order to purify himself, or even the tomb of Oinomaos himself, who wanted to torment the participants of the races. The name **Taraxippos**, is also attributed to Poseidon Hippios as an epithet. Other **Taraxippoi** are mentioned in Isthmia and in Nemea but it was the one at Olympia that panicked the horses the most.

The chariot races

The chariot races that were held in Olympia began with the **tethrippon** (quadriga) the oldest and most impressive race of this kind. It was introduced into the games in 680 BC (the 25th Olympiad). The chariot was a small wooden vehicle on two wooden wheels. It had enough space for two persons but, in contrast to what happened with the war chariots, during the races only one person was aboard. Four adult horses, 5 to 6 years old were yoked to the chariot. On the right hand side they would put the strongest and fastest horse in order to be able to take the turns more easily, as they were always left hand turns. In the races the **tethrippon** had to run twelve complete circuits of the racecourse, that is a distance corresponding to about 14 km.

The second race, in the order of their introduction into the Olympic Games, was the **apene**, which was introduced in 500 BC (the 70th Olympiad) but was abolished in 444 BC (the 84th Olympiad), because of lack of participants. The **apene** was a chariot pulled by two mules and the peculiarity of it was that the

A quadriga during the races. On the right the turning point or nyssa. In contrast to the athletes of the stadium the charioteer wears a long white gown (London, British Museum).

Apene. The chariot is being driven by a sitting charioteer (London, British Museum).

charioteer was seated during the race. The distance it had to cover was half that of the **tethrippon**; that is, about 7 km. The reason that this race was not popular was probably either that the mules are perverse animals and caused problems during the race or that they did not command the same respect as the horses. The superstitions in the area of Elis surrounding the breeders of mules illustrate this fact.

The **synoris**, included in the programme of the games from 408 BC (the 93rd Olympiad), was the same as the **apene** chariot but was pulled by two horses, which had to run six or eight times round the perimeter of the racecourse, that is 7 or 9 km.

The **tethrippon** for colts was introduced in 384 BC (the 99th Olympiad) and the **synoris** for colts in 268 BC (the 127th Olympiad) and ran round the race-course only three times (about 3.5 km). The classification of the horses into colts and fully-grown animals was done by the **Hellanodikai** after a short procedure.

The events on the racecourse and especially the chariot races were very dangerous, as we find out from the ancient writers, who talk about " horse wrecks" (Soph. - Electr.) with which the racecourse was filled. The most critical point was undoubtedly in front of the **nyssa**, which the charioteer tried to pass as close to as possible, in order to gain, the inside lane immediately after the turn. This was, of course, the aim of all the riders, therefore collisions were

A quadriga (Paris, Museum of the Louvre).

inevitable. Sophocles, in his "Electra", describes such an incident, where two chariots collided and the others, which were close behind, crashed one into the other. It is obvious how difficult the task of the charioteer was and how important his contribution was to the victory. It is thus strange that he only received a woolen band as a prize, which the horse trainer tied round his forehead, while the real prize of victory, the olive wreath, was given to the owner of the horses. This is the reason, as mentioned elsewhere, that children, women and even cities have been declared the winners of these races. It is true that several charioteers are still known in our times and that Pindar praises them in numerous odes, but the real glory of victory was not enjoyed by the ones who deserved it most.

A synoris on a golden coin of Philippos II after his victory in the chariot races (Athens,Coin Collection).

The horse races

Less popular than the chariot races were the horse races, which were also held on the racecourse. The ordinary horse race was introduced in 648 BC (the 33rd Olympiad) and the rider had to cover six lengths of the racecourse. In 256 BC (the 131st Olympiad) the horse race for colts was added, while from 496 up until 444 BC (the 71st to the 84th Olympiads), a rather strange race was added; the **kalpe** or mares race. The distance of the race is not clear but we know that for the last stretch the rider would dismount and run next to the horse, holding the reins, up to the finishing line.

The bronze complex of the jockey of Artemision (Athens, National Archaeological Museum).

A difference between the ancient and the modern horse races is that in those times they did not use horseshoes. It also seems that they did not use a saddle, although it was probably known to them, judging from a mention made by Xenophon (Peri Hipp. 7.5). However they did sometimes use stirrups with one sharp point and a whip.

The horses were very beloved animals to the ancient Greeks, who expressed this love in many ways. Many times they gave them names and some of them are known to us today, such as Phoenix, Korax, Parthenia, Samos etc. Sometimes they buried them in eye-catching tombs or took care to immortalize them as in the case of Pheidolas from Corinth's mare, Aura, which in spite of throwing her rider during the race, went on galloping and accelerated to the finishing line to take victory.

Scene of a horse race. The riders are nude and do not use a saddle (London, British Museum).

Silver inlaid depiction of a rider on a bronze helmet (Olympia, Archaeological Museum).

The Heraia

*H*era was the only divinity in Olympia who had the honour of being worshipped in a temple for about two centuries before the construction of the temple of Zeus, in the 5th century BC. The cult probably came to Olympia from Argos, where she was the main divinity and, to be precise, was introduced by the **tyrant** of the city, Pheidon, when, at the exhortation of the inhabitants of Pisa, he made an attempt to intervene in the sanctuary and to undertake the organization of the games (Herod. 6.127, Paus. 6.22.2). This theory is also supported by the coincidence of the time of the construction of the temple of Hera with the period of the sovereignty of Pheidon (7th century BC).

Pausanias (5.16.4), mentions Hippodameia as being the founder of the Heraia, together with sixteen women, one from each town of the area. These women had been chosen in order to resolve the difference between the Elians and the Pisatans and after having made peace, they enjoyed great respect. So, when Hippodameia wanted to thank Hera for her marriage to Pelops, she

Track race of women (Rome, Musei Vaticani).

Bronze statuette of a female athlete in track race (London, British Museum).

chose these women and together they organized a contest that from then on, took place every four years. This legend is obviously from posterity and does not prove the arguments of some scholars that the Heraia were older than the Olympic Games.

Although independent from the men's games, the Heraia were held in the same stadium, where the contestants had to run a course of 500 feet (160m), which corresponds to 5/6 of the track. The women who participated had to be virgins and ran after being divided into three categories according to their age. First the youngest, then the adolescents and finally the young women. They used to run with their hair loose, the tunic a little over the knees and the right shoulder naked to the breast. The prize was an olive wreath, a piece of meat from the cow that had been sacrificed to Hera and the right to put their image in the sanctuary. It should be noted that the meat that the winners were given was not a material reward but a way of deriving strength through eating from the sacrificial cow, a kind of communion.

Engraved depiction of a jumber on a discus (London, British Museum).

Bronze discus with engraved depiction of a javelin thrower. On the javelin the ankyle can be clearly distinguished (Berlin, Staatliche Museen)

The prizes

*I*n ancient Greece there were two kinds of games. The sacred or **stephanitai**, in which the prize was a **stephanos** (wreath) and the **thematikoi**, in which, beside the wreath they were also awarded **themata**, that is, objects of material worth or even money. These prizes varied from place to place. In Athens they were **amphoras** full of oil from the sacred olive tree of the goddess Athena, the patroness of the city; in Argos the prizes were shields and in other places, bronze receptacles, tripods, weapons or even clothes. These **thematikoi** games were always local and they were never esteemed as much as the **stephanitai**.

All four **panhellenic** games were **stephanitai**. In every sanctuary the wreath was made from branches of the sacred plant of the patron god of the area. In the Pythian Games it was a laurel wreath, in the Nemean it was from the celery plant, in the Isthmian games in the beginning it was a pine wreath and after the 5th century BC it was made of celery too. In the Olympic Games the wreath was always made from olive branches. A young man whose parents were still alive, would use a golden knife to cut some branches from the sacred wild olive tree of Zeus, that stood on the

Young athlete with the branches and the woolen bands of the winners (Leningrad, Hermitage Museum).

70

An agonothetes binds a band around the winner's head (Munich, Antikensammlungen)

southern side of the **opisthodomos** of the temple of Zeus and with them he used to weave the wreaths for the winners. Originally they were placed on a bronze tripod and then, after the 5th century BC on a precious gold and ivory table, the handiwork of the sculptor Kolotes, a pupil of Pheidias, which was kept in the **prodomos** of the temple of Zeus. The wreaths remained there until the last day of the games, when the coronation of the winners took place. And while the most senior member of the **Hellanodikai** placed the sacred wreaths on their heads, the spectators showered them with flowers. On the same evening, the winner's friends amused themselves with songs and chanted the Olympic Hymn, which the poet Archilochus from Paros had composed in honour of Hercules.

Another great honour for the athletes was that, after the victory, they were allowed to erect their statues in the **Altis**. And having their own images next to

The winner of a thematikos game. His prize, a tripod, is being carried by a young man. In front of him a herald announces the victory (London, British Museum).

ones of the gods was an extraordinary distinction, not only for the winners but also for their families and hometowns. This is the reason that in some cases it was the town that financed the construction of these monuments, on the pedestal of which, besides the winner's name, its own was immortalized. When Pausanias visited the sanctuary, in the 2nd century BC, he saw at least 230 such statues.

Sculpture was not the only art form employed in the immortalization of the athletes. Poetry was even more effective in spreading the fame of the Olympic winners abroad, because, as Pindar explains, the statues were seen only by those who visited the sanctuary, while the odes which praised the achievements of the winners circulated from mouth to mouth and were sung throughout the Greek world. This enormous fame that a victory ode assured explains the high amounts of money that the poets earned from its composition. This is why most of the odes were composed for winners of the chariot races, who were the wealthiest contestants but also for famous public personalities, such as the **tyrant** of Syracuse, Ieron. Immediately after the victory, the athlete or his relatives ordered an ode from the poet and when it was ready they would chant it outside the winner's house.

Many important ancient poets composed these odes that praise not only the achievements of the winner but also the athletic ideal. The most famous among them are Simonides from the island of Kea, (556-462 BC), his nephew Bacchylides (born around 524-521 BC) and the most important of all lyric poets of ancient Greece, Pindar from Thebes (518-438 BC).

Honouring the athletes was not restricted to the place where they had won. When they came back to their home town their compatriots honoured them in different ways. In Athens, the winners could eat for the rest of their life in the **Prytaneion**. They also had a seat of honour in the theatres of their town. In Sparta, during battle, they were given pride of place at the front,

Coin of Elis with representation of a winged victory holding a wreath (Athens, Coin Collection).

next to their king. In other towns their statues were erected in the market place or honourable plaques of stone or marble were constructed, on which the name of the winner as well as the event he had won were engraved. In other towns, on the return of the Olympionikai, their fellow citizens demolished a part of the city walls, through which the winners then entered, because they said that when a city has citizens who have won in the Olympic Games it has no need of fortification.

It is indeed very difficult for someone today to realize the significance that an Olympic victory had for the ancient Greeks. A slight inkling can probably be gained through the narration, by an ancient writer, of the story of Diagoras from Rhodes, winner in the **pankration**, who died in the stadium at Olympia, while being carried on the shoulders of his two sons, who had also just been crowned as winners. At that moment, a Spartan from the crowd of spectators shouted to him: «Die, Diagoras. All that is left for you to do is to go up to Olympus ". Having himself won at Olympia and having relived this triumph through his sons' victories, this was the most he could expect. It was the happiest moment of his life and for this reason the right one to die, as the beloved of the gods.

73

this fire, which with the passage of the time was considered sacred, is shown by the fact that its name **hestia**, which means fireplace, was given to one of the 12 gods of Olympus, **Hestia**, who was Zeus's sister and patron goddess of the house and the family. The same goddess was later called by the Romans Vesta and her sacred fire was kept in her temple, in the Forum Romanum, by six virgins, the Vestals. The same sacred fire is to be found in Christian churches, with the name ' the ever-burning fire'. At Olympia the sacred fire burned in the **Prytaneion**, a building at the N-W end of the **Altis**, built probably at the same period as the temple of Zeus. The **Prytaneion** was the centre of political life and of the administration of the sanctuary and the games. There, next to the hall with the fire, was the **hestiatorion** that is the hall of the **hestia**, where the Elians served the official meal to the winners of the games.

The meaning, then, of the Olympic flame today is that it becomes, symbolically, the centre around which, even for a few days all the people of the world will gather, in order to pay homage to the athletic ideal and peace, the way the ancient Greeks did for twelve centuries. And even if it sounds utopian in our day and age, the power of some ideals is immense. Let us not underestimate that in ancient Greece, what the politicians did not achieve for centuries, the unification of the independent city-states, was essentially accomplished by the games at Olympia.

Pausanias

A n ancient writer, whom the reader of this book will often come across is Pausanias. He lived in the 2nd century AD and is well-known for one of his works, the "Periegesis (or A Guide) to Greece". It is quite a long text (it has more words than the Iliad and the Odyssey put together), divided into 10 books, each one named after a different province of Greece, with the exception of Elis, the area where Olympia was situated, to which he dedicates two books. This work of Pausanias does not have any literary value but it gives us a detailed description of the sanctuaries and the most important towns of his time. The narration is based on personal experience as well as on second-hand information, especially as far as religious beliefs and traditions are concerned, of which he seems to have been fond. The extensive description of monuments, temples and works of art has very often helped modern excavators in the identification of their findings and makes the " Periegesis" a unique and irreplaceable source of information.

Theodosius I

522 and 551   Destruction of the buildings by earthquakes.

1829   First attempts to locate and excavate the monuments.

1875   Beginning of the systematic excavations.

1896   The first modern Olympic Games.

BIBLIOGRAPHY

Ancient Writers

Athenaios	Deipnosophistes (Supper sophists)
Aristophanes	Hippeis (Riders)
Aristotle	Physics, Rhetoric, Politics, The Athenian Republic
Dion	Chryssostomos Demegoria (Public Orators)
Galen	
Homer	The Iliad, The Odyssey
Lucian	Anacharsis, Ermotimos
Lysias	Olympic Speech
Pausanias	A Guide To Greece
Philostratos	Gymnastikos (Gymnastics), Eikones (Pictures)
Pindar	Epiniki (Victory Celebrations)
Plato	The Laws, The Republic
Plutarch	Parallel Lives, Symposium, Ethics
Sophocles	Electra
Thucydides	History of the peloponnesian war
Xenophon	Peri Hippikes, Apomnemoneumata (Recollections)

Modern Authors

Curtius, E., Adler F.,	Olympia, die Ergebnisse, 5 vol., Berlin 1966
Gardiner, E.N.,	Athletics in the Ancient World, Oxford 1930
»	Greek Athletic Sports and Festivals, London 1910
Harris, H.A.,	Greek Athletes and the Athletics, London 1964 republished by Ares publishers Inc. Chicago 1978
»	Sport in Greece and Rome, London 1972
Mallwitz, A.,	
Hermann, H.V.,	Die Funde aus Olympia, Athen 1980
Yalouris, N.,	Ancient Olympia and the Olympic Games, Athens 1977

GLOSSARY

agon   fight, struggle. Game

agon stephanites   game with a wreath as a prize

agon thematikos   game with material prize

akoniti   without dust. The way of winning a game without having fought

Altis   grove. The name of the sanctuary at Olympia

amphora   vase with two handles

ankyle   leather strap which was bound like a handle around the spear

apagoreuein   concede my defeat in a game

apene   chariot pulled by two mules

aphetes   the one who gave the signal for the start of the events

aulos   musical instrument, kind of flute

balbis   place from which the throws of the disc and the javelin were made. starting line of the courses

barbarian   barbarian anyone who was not Greek and whose language was not comprehensible and thus sounded like 'bar- bar'.

bater   fixed board of stone or wood, where the athletes stepped before making a jump.

Boule, Bouleuterion   the parliament. The building that was the seat of the deputies.

diaulos   double flute. A course that covered twice the length of the stadium, corresponding to the modern 400 m.

dolichos   long-distance race, 7 to 24 stadia long, corresponding to the 1500 to 5000 m of today.

ephedros	the athlete who proceeded to the next round of the event without having fought.
epotides	protective covers of the ears, that the boxers wore during training.
Gaia	earth. One of the names of the prehistoric goddess of fertility.
gymnasion	building where the men used to train naked.
gymnos	nude, naked.
halteres	weights that the athletes used during the jump
hecatombe	sacrifice of one hundred oxen, the biggest ritual of the ancient Greek religion.
Hestia	fire place. One of the twelve gods of Olympus, patron goddess of the house and the family.
hestiatorion	the room where the fire place was located. A hall in the **Prytaneion**, where the official meals were served. The restaurant.
himantes	straps that the athletes bound around the hands.
hippodrome	the track on which the horses used to run. The racecourse.
hippos	the horse.
kampter	small column or post, that marked the turning point of the races in the stadium.
kanon	wooden pole, with which they used to measure the jumps and the throws.
koryx	sack full of sand, for the training of the athletes.
kotinos	the olive wreath with which the winners of the games were crowned.
Kronion	the hill on the northern side of Olympia, named after the god Kronos, father of Zeus.
Krypte	hidden. The name of the covered entrance of the stadium of Olympia.

nyssa	the turning point for the horses and the chariots, in the racecourse.
Olympus	the highest mountain of Greece, residence of the twelve gods. (The Olympic gods)
olympionikes	the winner of the Olympic games.
opisthodomos	a part of the temple, behind the central hall or **sekos** (cella).
palaistra	building for the training of the athletes in the wrestling.
pale	the wrestling.
pale orthia	standing wrestling
pale kato	floor wrestling
panhellenic	for all the **Hellenes** (Greeks).
pankratiastes	athlete of the **pankration**.
pankration	sports event, a combination of wrestling and boxing.
pentathlon	five events. A composite event consisting of **stadion**, jump, discus, javelin and wrestling.
prodomos	the entrance hall of the temple, before the **sekos** (cella).
Prytaneion	the seat of the Prytaneis. Building in the sanctuary, with the altar of **Hestia**, where the eternal flame burned
sekos	the central part of the temple, where the cult statue stood.
semata	wooden pegs with which they marked the jumps and the throws.
skamma	sand-pit. The place where the wrestling, the boxing and the **pankration** were held but also where the athletes jumped.
skiamachia	shadow boxing. A form of training for the boxers.

stadion	a) the place where the games were held. b) the single race, one length of the track, corresponding to the modern 200m race. c) a measure of length, corresponding to 192.27m.
stlegis	metallic tool, with which the athletes cleaned their body from the dust and oil after the games.
synoris	chariot pulled by two horses quadriga.
Taraxippos	the one who agitates the horses. Altar dedicated to an unknown divinity who caused panic to the horses.
tethrippon	chariot pulled by four horses. Quadriga.
tyrant	title of a sovereign. Because most of them were not popular, the word today has negative connotations.
Zeus	the father of the gods and men, according to mythology.

CONTENS

Reconstruction of the Altis. In the centre the Metroon, on the left the treasuries and in the background the entrance of the stadium (after E. Curtius, Olympia, Archaeological Museum).